What's
Beneath
Our Cities?

Adam Ford

What's Beneath Our Cities?

Text: Adam Ford
Publishers: Tania Mazzeo and Eliza Webb
Series consultant: Amanda Sutera
  Hands on Heads Consulting
Editor: Sarah Layton
Project Editor: Annabel Smith
Designer: Leigh Ashforth
Project designer: Danielle Maccarone
Permissions researcher: Liz McShane
Production controller: Renee Tome

Acknowledgements
We would like to thank the following for permission to reproduce copyright material:

Front cover: iStock.com/LeoPatrizi; pp. 1, 4: iStock.com/eduardod; pp. 3, 6, 10, 14, 18, 24 (skyline vector images): iStock.com/Greens87; p. 5 (top left): iStock.com/Yiran An, (top right): iStock.com/saiko3p, (bottom left): Shutterstock.com/S.Borisov, (bottom right): iStock.com/OlegAlbinsky; p. 6: Mitchell Library, State Library of New South Wales; p. 7 (main): Federated Builders' Association of Australia & Master Builders' Federation of Australia. (1907). Building: the magazine for the architect, builder, property owner and merchant Retrieved November 30, 2023, from http://nla.gov.au/nla.obj-79483170, (inset): Mitchell Library, State Library of New South Wales; p. 8: Dan Crisp © Cengage Learning Australia Pty Limited; p. 9 (main): Alamy Stock Photo/Erik Schlogl; pp. 9 (inset), back cover (bottom): Busby's Bore under Oxford Street Darlinghurst, circa 1830 (01/01/1824 - 31/12/1837), [A-00069725]. City of Sydney Archives, accessed 30 Nov 2023, https://archives.cityofsydney.nsw.gov.au/nodes/view/696101; p. 10: Alamy Stock Photo/PWB Images; p. 11: Alamy Stock Photo/SPCOLLECTION; p. 12 (main): Alamy Stock Photo/Classic Image, (inset): Shutterstock.com/ttomasek15; p. 13 (top): Alamy Stock Photo/dpa picture alliance, (bottom): Getty Images/DOMINIQUE FAGET; p. 14: Alamy Stock Photo/Chronicle; p. 15: Science Photo Library/George Bernard; p. 16 (main): Getty Images/Hulton Deutsch, (inset): Alamy Stock Photo/World History Archive; p. 17 (main): Getty Images/Jack Taylor, (inset): Shutterstock.com/Anatoliy Sadovskiy; p. 18: Alamy Stock Photo/Gado Images; p. 19: Alamy Stock Photo/Penta Springs Limited; p. 20 (main): iStock.com/aluxum, (inset): Shutterstock.com/Evannovostro; p. 21: iStock.com/eugenesergeev; p. 22, back cover (top): iStock.com/Straitel.

Every effort has been made to trace and acknowledge copyright. However, if any infringement has occurred, the publishers tender their apologies and invite the copyright holders to contact them.

NovaStar

ISBN 978 0 17 033431 0

Cengage Learning Australia
Level 5, 80 Dorcas Street
Southbank VIC 3006 Australia
Phone: 1300 790 853
Email: aust.nelsonprimary@cengage.com

For learning solutions, visit **cengage.com.au**

Printed in China by 1010 Printing International Ltd
1 2 3 4 5 6 7 28 27 26 25 24

Nelson acknowledges the Traditional Owners and Custodians of the lands of all First Nations Peoples. We pay respect to Elders past and present, and extend that respect to all First Nations Peoples today.

Contents

Hidden Surprises

Beneath most cities lie millions of kilometres of pipes, electrical wires, and tunnels for underground trains. But other more surprising things have lain hidden, sometimes for hundreds of years, beneath the hustle and bustle of city streets.

The London Underground is a large system of trains that runs beneath the city.

In this book, you'll read about some very different but very important **structures** that lie beneath four world-famous cities.

Sydney

Paris

London

New York City

Busby's Bore, Sydney

Busby's Bore is a tunnel that was cut through solid rock under the **colonial** town of Sydney, Australia, between 1827 and 1837. It was built to solve a serious problem that threatened the lives of the people of Sydney. They didn't have enough fresh, clean water!

The original water supply for the early settlement of Sydney was a river called the Tank Stream. But, as the community grew along its banks, the Tank Stream became very polluted and the water was undrinkable. The town needed a new **source** of clean water.

The Tank Stream was filled with waste from people and animals.

The bore, which is another word for a hole or tunnel, was designed by an **engineer** named John Busby. Busby came up with a plan to dig a tunnel from Hyde Park, in the centre of the town, through a sandstone hill to a freshwater **spring** called Lachlan Swamps. The tunnel took water from the spring and directed it into the town, where it could be used for drinking and washing.

John Busby, 1836

This plan for Busby's Bore shows its path from Lachlan Swamps (far right) to Hyde Park (far left).

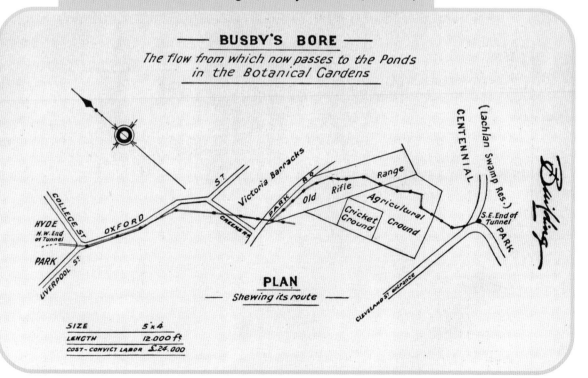

BUSBY'S BORE

The flow from which now passes to the Ponds in the Botanical Gardens

PLAN
Shewing its route

SIZE — 5' x 4'
LENGTH — 12,000 ft
COST - CONVICT LABOR — £24,000

The construction of Busby's Bore took 10 years and was a difficult and dangerous job. The workers, who were all **convicts**, had to dig through solid rock by candlelight with just hand tools. They also had to face life-threatening events, such as flooding and cave-ins of the tunnel. They even had to change the direction of the tunnel to avoid **quicksand**, which was not safe to dig through.

Despite these challenges, the bore was completed in 1837, and it quickly became an important source of water for the city. The water was clean and fresh, and it helped to prevent diseases like **cholera** and **typhoid** that had been a big problem in the past.

Building Busby's Bore

This is an artist's imagining of convicts digging Busby's Bore while John Busby watches from above ground.

Busby's Bore supplied Sydney's **population** with up to 1.5 million litres of clean water a day. It remained the main water supply for Sydney until 1859.

Today, Busby's Bore is still part of Sydney's water supply, and it does important work in providing clean water to Sydney's Botanic Gardens.

a side tunnel in Busby's Bore

Traditional Owners of the Land

Busby's Bore was built through lands belonging to the Bidjigal and Gadigal First Nations peoples, on the area now known as Lachlan Swamps. The Gadigal people are the **Traditional Owners of the Land** on which the city of Sydney sits today.

The Paris Catacombs

The Paris catacombs are tunnels underneath the streets of Paris, the capital city of France. The tunnels were once **quarries**, or places where stone was dug up to build the city. But in the late 1700s, they were used to overcome a big problem: the city's cemeteries were full!

During the 1700s, the population of Paris grew very quickly. Too many people were living, and dying, in Paris, and the old cemeteries were running out of room. At the city's central cemetery, so many bodies had been buried on top of one another that the land was 2 metres higher than surrounding streets! There was also a risk of disease spreading from the human **remains** that lay just below the surface.

Something had to be done!

Paris's central cemetery was the oldest in the city and one of the most overcrowded.

Beginning in 1786, human remains were dug up by workers from the cemeteries and moved to the underground tunnels. The bones were taken through the streets in black cloth-covered wagons at night to avoid alarming the people of Paris. It took 2 years to move most of the bones into the old tunnels. These tunnels would become the catacombs.

About the Word

The word "catacomb" comes from an Old English word that means "underground cemetery".

Remains were removed from Paris's main cemetery from 1786 to 1788.

Over time, the skeletons of more than 6 million people were moved to the catacombs. In the beginning, the bones were piled high in a huge jumble. But starting in 1810, they were assembled in unusual and surprising ways. The reason was to create a **memorial** to the dead that people could visit. Skulls and other bones from human skeletons were arranged to form patterned walls of bones that reached to the ceilings.

Cross symbols are used throughout the catacombs to create smaller memorials.

Once the catacombs were full, they became a popular tourist attraction. People from all over the world came to see the underground tunnels and the bones that were stacked inside. But by the end of the 1800s, the catacombs were all but forgotten.

Construction of the catacombs memorial continued in 1866 while visitors looked on.

During World War II, the catacombs found a different use as a hiding place for people in the **French Resistance**. They used the tunnels to move around the city without being seen by the German soldiers, who had taken control of Paris.

German troops ride through Paris's streets in 1940.

In recent times, the catacombs have again become a popular spot for adventurous tourists and people looking for an unusual location to have parties. In 2004, Paris police even discovered a cinema – complete with a screen, rolls of film and seats for an audience – inside the catacombs.

However, the catacombs are dangerous to explore, and many people have become lost or injured while trying to find their way around the spooky tunnels. It is illegal to enter the catacombs without a guide, so if you want to visit, it is best to go with a tour guide.

More than half a million tourists visit the Paris catacombs each year.

The London Sewers

Sewers are pipes and tunnels built under the ground to carry away waste, also known as "sewerage", from our toilets. Sewers may do an unpleasant job, but they are very important for keeping cities clean and healthy.

In the past, sewers often leaked or emptied waste into rivers. Many places did not have any sewers at all, and waste flowed into the streets. This made city life very smelly – and dangerous, as deadly diseases could spread if sewerage got into drinking water. In the 1800s, London, England, had a big sewerage problem in its main river, the Thames.

The Thames River flows through central London in 1854.

London's population had grown very quickly. Its old sewer system was not built for the number of people living there. This resulted in a lot of sewerage flowing into the Thames River. In the summer of 1858, the river was so full of sewerage that it created a terrible smell. People called it the "Great Stink". After that, the government decided that London needed a new sewer system.

Many people protested against sewerage in the Thames River, as shown in this comic drawing from 1828.

London's new sewer system was built between 1859 and 1870. It was designed by an engineer called Joseph Bazalgette. Bazalgette planned and built a **network** of tunnels under London that would safely carry the waste from thousands of toilets away from the city.

Joseph Bazalgette, 1887

The new system was a huge project that took 11 years to complete. Bazalgette's team of thousands of workers dug more than 1700 kilometres of **drains** and 130 kilometres of tunnels that were so large that a person could easily walk through them.

Joseph Bazalgette (at top right of image) visited part of the sewer while it was under construction.

Bazalgette's sewer made a big difference to the city of London. The streets were cleaner, and the air was fresher. People were much healthier, as the new system almost **eliminated** diseases like cholera, which had killed thousands of people in the past.

Amazingly, Bazalgette's sewers are still in use today!

Brick by Brick

Around 318 million bricks were used to build London's new sewer system.

The London sewer system is still in use today.

The New York City Steam System

Manhattan is the name of an island and one of the most famous boroughs, or areas, of New York City, USA. Underneath its city streets is an underground system of pipes that carry hot steam between the boroughs of Brooklyn and Queens and back to the island of Manhattan. The steam is made in huge **boilers** at power stations. It helps keep the city warm in the winter as it flows through pipes and **radiators** in buildings.

Before the steam system was built in the late 1800s, people burned coal or wood to heat the homes and businesses that crowded the small island. Smoke from the thousands of fireplaces caused choking pollution. The possibility of these fires getting out of control and burning down buildings or neighbourhoods was a constant threat.

The island of Manhattan was very overcrowded in the 1800s.

A steam system was a much better solution, because the fires that heated the boilers could be kept away from the crowded neighbourhoods. The boilers turned water into steam, just like giant kettles!

Construction of the underground steam system began in the 1870s and was completed in 1882. It was a very big job that involved laying over 160 kilometres of metal pipes under the streets of Manhattan. The pipes were then connected to more than 1700 homes and businesses, including the famous Empire State Building skyscraper.

Workers laid the steam system pipes under the streets of New York City.

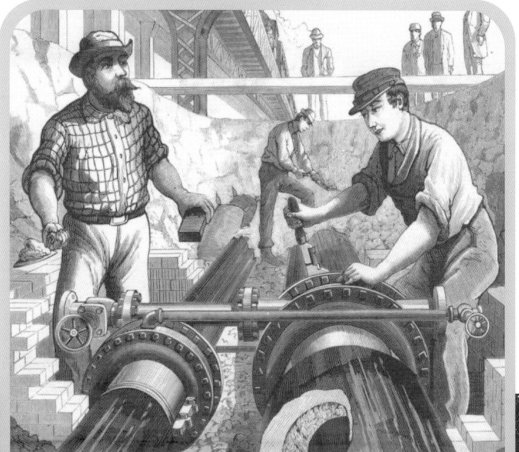

Today, Manhattan's steam system heats schools, hospitals and museums, as well as hundreds of homes. But the steam is not just used for heating. It is also used to cook food in many restaurants, clean dirty dishes and even steam-clean clothes.

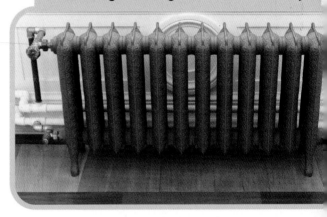

Steam radiators can still be found in buildings throughout New York City.

Occasionally, the pipes crack and big clouds of white steam billow into the air from **grills** in the streets and footpaths.

A cloud of steam comes up through a grill in the street.

A Steamy Solution

Using steam to heat buildings is a very old idea. Two thousand years ago, during the **Roman Empire,** buildings such as public bath houses were heated by steam that was produced in boilers and flowed through spaces under floors.

The Roman Baths in the city of Bath, England, (built around 70 AD) are heated by an underground steam system.

Over time, the way the New York City steam system works has been improved, and it is better for the environment. Today, the system is still an important part of Manhattan, more than 140 years after it was first built.

Look Down!

So much of city life cannot go on without the hidden structures that lie beneath our streets and buildings. These structures help to keep the air clean, keep the water fresh, and make sure we are safe and warm.

Next time you are in a city, look down and imagine what lies beneath your feet!

Glossary

boilers (*noun*) — containers where water is heated to make steam

cholera (*noun*) — a deadly illness caused by infected water

colonial (*adjective*) — having to do with a colony – a place that has been settled by people from another country

convicts (*noun*) — prisoners found guilty of a crime

drains (*noun*) — pipes that carry away dirty water

eliminated (*verb*) — got rid of something

engineer (*noun*) — someone who makes machines or buildings

French Resistance (*noun*) — people living in France who fought against German control of the country in World War II

grills (*noun*) — flat metal frames that air can pass through

memorial (*noun*) — a statue or location built to remember people who have died

network (*noun*) — lots of connected paths

population (*noun*) — the number of people living in a certain place

quarries (*noun*) — big pits in the ground where stone is dug up

quicksand (*noun*) — deep, wet sand that people can sink into

radiators (*noun*) — heating systems made up of pipes that hot water or steam passes through

remains (*noun*) — bodies of dead people

Roman Empire (*noun*) — a group of countries that were controlled by a single emperor in Ancient Rome

source (*noun*) — a place that you get something from

spring (*noun*) — a place where water, usually clean, flows up from underground

structures (*noun*) — buildings or other objects that have been built from different parts

Traditional Owners (*noun*) — the people who have lived on and cared for the land for a long time

typhoid (*noun*) — a deadly illness caused by infected food or water

Index